HEALTH MATTERS

KEEPING CLEAN AND HEALTHY

Nancy Dickmann

Published by Brown Bear Books Ltd
4877 N. Circulo Bujia
Tucson, AZ 85718
USA

and

G14, Regent Studios
1 Thane Villas
London N7 7PH
UK

© 2025 Brown Bear Books Ltd

ISBN 978-1-83572-008-0 (ALB)
ISBN 978-1-83572-014-1 (paperback)
ISBN 978-1-83572-020-2 (ebook)

All rights reserved. No part of this book may be reproduced, stored in a retrieval system, or transmitted, in any form or by any means, electronic, mechanical, photocopying, recording, or otherwise, without the prior written permission of the copyright holder.

Library of Congress Cataloging-in-Publication Data available on request

Designer: Trudi Webb
Design Manager: Keith Davis
Children's Publisher: Anne O'Daly
Picture Manager: Sophie Mortimer

Picture Credits
Cover: Shutterstock: lemono and Shutterstock Vector Stock Library.
Interior: Shutterstock: Tess Brunet 12, domitoon 11, Lala Firden 6, GoodStudio 14, 19, Iconic Bestiary 15, Inspiring 20, Kakigori Studio 13, lemono 1, Macro Vector 5, Antonov Maxim 8, mhatzapa 21, Marina Naumova 9, PCH Vector 10, Amanita Silvicora 16, sycamore 4, Tenstudio 7, 18, Ksenia Zvedina 17.

All other artwork, Brown Bear Books and Shutterstock Vector Stock Library.

Brown Bear Books has made every attempt to contact the copyright holder.
If you have any information about omissions, please contact: licensing@brownbearbooks.co.uk

Manufactured in the United States of America
CPSIA compliance information: Batch#AG/5662

Websites
The website addresses in this book were valid at the time of going to press. However, it is possible that contents or addresses may change following publication of this book. No responsibility for any such changes can be accepted by the author or the publisher. Readers should be supervised when they access the Internet.

Contents

Personal Hygiene 4

Germ Alert! 6

Bath Time 8

Clean Hair 10

Skin and Nails 12

Healthy Teeth 14

Wash Your Hands! 16

Stopping Germs 18

Clean Clothes 20

Your Turn! 22

Find Out More 22

Glossary 23

Index 24

Personal Hygiene

Grown-ups often talk about good hygiene. But what does that mean?

Personal hygiene is about keeping yourself clean and healthy. It means taking care of your own body. Good hygiene keeps you looking and smelling good. It helps keep you from getting sick.

Babies need help keeping clean. But you can be in charge of your own personal hygiene.

Sometimes getting dirty can be a lot of fun!

Why Hygiene Matters

Good hygiene helps you feel confident. Knowing that you look and smell your best can make you feel good. It's still OK to get dirty or sweaty when you play. But take the time to clean up afterward. This shows that you care about your body.

What's in a Name?

Our word "hygiene" comes from the Greek goddess Hygieia. She was a goddess of health and cleanliness.

Germ Alert!

Hygiene isn't just about looking good. It's also about stopping germs.

Germs are tiny living things. There are two main types. They are bacteria and viruses. Some bacteria and viruses are helpful. They help digest food. Or they make soil better for farming. But some kinds are harmful. They cause disease. We call them germs.

Germs are too small to see without a microscope.

Spreading Germs

We can't see germs. But germs are all around. They are tiny enough to float in the air. They might be in water and other liquids. If germs get into your body, they can make you ill. Good hygiene helps keep germs out.

A grain of salt is tiny. But **100** bacteria could line up along its side. It would take **1,000** viruses to do the same!

grain of salt

bacteria

Pinkeye is a common illness. It's caused by germs getting into the lining of the eye.

Bath Time

How can you keep your body clean?
Take a bath or shower!

Some people bathe every day. Others do it a few times a week. There's no rule about it. It depends on how active you are! Do you do a lot of sports or playing outside? That makes you sweaty or dirty. You might need to bathe more often.

Taking a hot bath is a great way to relax!

There are lots of soaps and body washes to choose from. Some are good for people with sensitive skin.

Getting Clean

Use a washcloth or sponge to gently rub away any dirt. Then use soap or shower gel to wash your arms and legs. Wash under your arms and between your toes. You also need to carefully wash your bottom. Don't forget your face and neck!

After you wash your body, what's the next step?

A. make sure the water is not too hot

B. rinse off any suds

C. get undressed and hop in the tub

Clean Hair

Hair can be straight or curly, kinky or smooth. It all needs taking care of!

When you bathe, wet your hair and then lather it up with shampoo. Make sure to rub it gently into your scalp. Then rinse away the suds. You should comb or brush your hair every day, even if you don't take a bath.

Conditioner
Some people use conditioner after shampoo. It makes their hair softer and easier to manage.

A haircut trims off any damaged ends. It keeps your hair healthy and looking good.

Having head lice can make your head itchy. But it won't make you sick.

Head Lice

Head lice are tiny bugs that can live on your scalp. Anyone can get head lice. It doesn't matter if your hair is clean or dirty. Lice are passed on by touching heads or sharing hats or hairbrushes. An adult can help you get rid of them. They'll use special shampoo and combs.

Skin and Nails

Good hygiene includes taking care of your nails and skin.

Washing your skin in the bath is a great first step. Make sure to dry it gently with a towel afterward. If your skin dries out, lotion will help keep it soft. Sometimes skin gets itchy or flaky. Ask an adult to help you get it checked out.

The sun can hurt your skin. Always wear sunscreen when playing out in the sun.

Healthy Nails

Fingernails are really useful. It's important to keep them in good shape. Keep them clean and neatly trimmed. And don't forget your toenails. Nails are softer and easier to cut right after a bath. If you're not sure how to trim them yourself, an adult can help you.

Biting your nails is a bad idea. It can hurt your teeth or nails and spread germs.

Fingernails grow about **0.1 inches (3.5 mm)** per month. That's about twice the width of a piece of dried spaghetti!

Healthy Teeth

You use your teeth every day.
They need to stay healthy and strong.

Your teeth get covered in plaque. Plaque is a sticky film. It has food, spit, and germs in it. Brushing your teeth helps remove it. A brush cleans the tops and sides of your teeth. Dental floss cleans between them.

Brush your teeth in the morning and again before bed. Brush for two minutes each time.

Cavities

Too much plaque can make holes in your teeth. These are called cavities. A dentist can fix most cavities by putting a filling in. But the best plan is to prevent them. Good brushing will help. Make sure you don't eat too much sugar.

> **Sugary foods and drinks damage teeth. Which of these contain sugar?**
> A. candy bar
> B. fruit juice
> C. cake
> D. all of the above

Dentists check that your teeth are healthy. Visit your dentist at least once a year.

Wash Your Hands!

Keeping your hands clean is one of the most important parts of personal hygiene.

Think of all the ways you use your hands. You pick up things at the store. You wipe your bottom after using the toilet. You pat animals and prepare food. Hands pick up germs all the time. The germs get into your body when you eat or touch your face.

Exploring nature is fun, but always wash your hands afterward.

Make It Count

Wash your hands before eating or cooking. Wash them again after using the toilet or touching anything dirty. Just rinsing your hands won't kill germs. Wash them with soap and water. Make sure to get between your fingers too.

Wash for at least 20 seconds. Time it by singing "Happy Birthday" twice!

Which of these activities will make you need to wash your hands?
A. watching a show on TV
B. helping weed the garden
C. taking a shower

Stopping Germs

How can you keep yourself from spreading germs?

Washing your hands helps protect you from germs. But what if you're the one spreading them? Colds and other illnesses are easy to pass on. Always cover your mouth when you cough or sneeze. That keeps germs from spraying into the air.

Blow your nose into a tissue. Then throw the tissue away and wash your hands.

Older people catch germs more easily. You can protect them by practicing good hygiene.

A single sneeze can send **100,000** germs into the air!

Stop the Spread

Sharing is good, but not if it means sharing germs too! Never share water bottles or eating utensils. Don't share towels, either. Sharing these things might pass on germs. If you're sick, stay at home if you can. You don't want to pass it on to anyone else.

Clean Clothes

It's not just hands that can spread germs. Clothes can carry germs, too.

You should change your socks and underwear every day. Other clothes don't need washing quite as often. You can wear jeans or shorts a few times between washes. The same goes for sweaters and hoodies. But if they smell or look dirty, toss them in the wash!

Washing clothes for a family is a big job. Could you help?

Clean and Healthy

Clean clothes smell nice. They often feel nice and soft, too! Wearing clean clothes can help you feel good about yourself. It can also keep you healthy! Washing clothes gets rid of stains. It can also kill germs, especially if you use hot water.

Washing Clothes
Some people wash clothes every day. Washing too often wears out your clothes.

Drying clothes outside saves energy.
The sunlight also kills many kinds of germs.

Your Turn!

You can take charge of your personal hygiene! Here are some ideas.

1. Make a chart to plan how often you will brush your teeth, wash your hands, take a bath, and wash your clothes. How well did you do?
2. Can you help your family improve their personal hygiene? Why not make a poster to explain why it's important to wash your hands? Hang it where everyone will see it.

Find Out More

Books

Connors, Kathleen. *I Stay Clean! (Healthy Me!)*. New York: Gareth Stevens, 2022.

Mansfield, Nicole A. *Keeping Your Teeth Clean (My Teeth)*. Mankato, Minn.: Capstone Publishing, 2023.

Woolley, Katie. *Keeping Clean (My Healthy Life)*. New York: Rosen Publishing, 2024.

Websites

www.healthforkids.co.uk/staying-healthy/looking-after-my-teeth/

kidshealth.org/en/kids/wash-hands.html

www.wonderopolis.org/wonder/how-clean-can-our-bodies-get

Glossary

bacteria tiny living things; some types are helpful while others can cause disease

conditioner a kind of lotion used to keep hair soft, shiny, and healthy

confident having faith in your own abilities and feeling good about yourself

dental floss a kind of wax-covered thread used to clean between the teeth

digest to break food down into the materials and nutrients that can be used by the body

electricity a form of energy that flows as a current, which we can use to power devices

germs a name we use for various kinds of tiny living things that cause illness

head lice small, wingless insects that sometimes live in the hair, where they lay eggs

personal hygiene the practice of keeping yourself clean to stay healthy and avoid illness

plaque a sticky, colorless film that forms on teeth and that can cause cavities if it's not removed by brushing and flossing

scalp the skin on the top and back of the head, which is usually covered in hair

viruses tiny living things that enter the body and cause illnesses such as colds and flu

Index

B
bacteria 6, 7
bathing 8, 9, 10
biting nails 13

C
cavities 15
clothes 20, 21

D
dirt 9

F
feeling good 5, 21
fingernails 13

G
germs 6, 7, 14, 16, 17, 18, 19, 20, 21
getting dirty or sweaty 5, 8
getting sick 4, 7, 11, 19

H
hair 10, 11
head lice 11
hygiene 4, 5, 6, 7, 12, 16, 19

L
looking good 4, 5, 6, 10

P
pinkeye 7
plaque 14, 15

S
skin 9, 12
soap 9, 17
spreading germs 18, 19
sugary foods 15
sun 12

T
teeth 14, 15
toenails 13

U
using the toilet 16, 17

V
viruses 6

W
washing hands 16, 17, 18

Answers to questions

page 9: B (checking the water temperature and hopping in the tub happen at the beginning of your bath, before you wash your hair)

page 15: D (candy bars, fruit juice, and cake all contain lots of sugar, so don't have too much, and brush your teeth afterward)

page 17: B (soil can be full of bacteria; taking a shower gets you clean and sitting quietly watching TV shouldn't make your hands dirty, unless you're also patting a pet or picking your nose!)